# HINDSIGHT
## 20/40

*poems and photographs by*

# Liz Whiteacre

*Finishing Line Press*
Georgetown, Kentucky

*Snake plant sunning in the living room*

# HINDSIGHT
## 20/40

Copyright © 2026 by Liz Whiteacre
ISBN 979-8-89990-345-8 First Edition
All rights reserved under International and Pan-American Copyright Conventions. No part of this book may be reproduced in any manner whatsoever without written permission from the publisher, except in the case of brief quotations embodied in critical articles and reviews.

Publisher: Leah Huete de Maines
Editor: Christen Kincaid
Cover Art: Liz Whiteacre
Interior Photos: Liz Whiteacre
Author Photo: Lee Hull Moses (2024) & Robert F. Schmidt (1998)
Cover Design: Elizabeth Maines McCleavy

Order online: www.finishinglinepress.com
also available on amazon.com

Author inquiries and mail orders:
Finishing Line Press
PO Box 1626
Georgetown, Kentucky 40324
USA

# Contents

| | |
|---|---|
| 01 | Hindsight Is 20/40 |
| 02 | Upon Closing My Eyes / @ 20 |
| 03 | At Dawn, Eyes Open / @ 40 |
| 04 | The Spin Cycle / @ 20 |
| 05 | Hang Dry / @ 40 |
| 07 | Trichromatic Theory of Seeing |
| 10 | Dancing Silver Fish / @ 20 |
| 14 | Unobstructed Koi / @ 40 |
| 16 | The Day My Dog Died / @ 20 |
| 17 | the day our cat died / reflecting @ 40 |
| 19 | (nearsighted) |
| 20 | Cycles on Wood Street / @ 20 |
| 22 | Cycles on Wind Street / @ 40 |
| 24 | Rush Hour Rant / @ 20 |
| 25 | Deck Dining Rant / @ 40 |
| 27 | night vision |
| 29 | @ 20 / So do you use safe sex? |
| 32 | @ 40 / Don't you think she's dressed like a whore? |
| 34 | 87° F / @ 20 |
| 35 | 98.6° F / @ 40 |
| 37 | TBD |
| 38 | Portrait of Longing on Highway 31 / @ 20 |
| 39 | Portrait of Mourning in the Coop / @ 40 |
| 42 | Wedding Ring Pattern / @ 20 |
| 43 | Log Cabin Pattern / @ 40 |
| 45 | Electrical impulses, that's all |
| | |
| 46 | Acknowledgments |
| 47 | Author Bio |

*Bee in the summer penstemons*

*for Hattie @18*

*Swamp oak has nearly dropped its leaves, our sign of spring*

# Hindsight Is 20/40

20/

If Herman Snellen stuck his first three-color photograph, possibly of his first love, to his wall, paced twenty feet, and turned back, was his L O V E still in focus? What if those slow steps, moving away from L O V E and place and time, measured by the size of his boots, distorted his L O V E ? Would he have hesitated after his pivot and moved closer, until he saw what he wanted? Or continued backstepping, slowly, letting L O V E become, if not clearer, perhaps fuzzier, nostalgic, warped?

/40

I found the binder of old poems in an office box, hauled state to state. Newly settled, I touched the paper my 20/year/old hands had hole punched and bound. It is hard to read those poems without a red pen—to suppress the desire to clean, reshape, brighten the fuzzy, forgotten feelings and memories now part of new narratives—scoping clarity like the optometrist's flipping of lenses: 1or2? now 2or3? now 3or4? –or1? I imagine Snellen's Eye Test, its 20 paces, my choices blurring, overlapping on the page, the decades-old text the only thing in sharp focus.

/

I will not understand this compulsion to write to my younger self until /60.

## Upon Closing My Eyes / @ 20

everything in my head is a story
impaired
my mind is snipped at by scissors
until all that is left

of my concentration
are perfect paper dolls dancing furiously in circles
paper cuts on my index finger
sting from touching the white
smooth hands that clutch each other

entwined like barbed wire
a menace to real girls
ponytails hurt when mothers
brush and tug
tying ribbons
that collide
bright and out of place

eluding me as though I walk naked down a crowded street—
oh, what rests in my head—
I soar, as grease, which sweats
off sizzling bacon careening
off clouds in the clear night
clouds as soft to my skin as flannel

leaves float falling with the hurt in my head
while midnight's yin yang struggles
like the globe to turn in the sky

a brilliant breast dancing upon the center of the ocean—
round reflected
as candy in the eye of a child—

a bright smear in my mind
like cinnamon passing over the tongue
scalding sweet

I bite the moon
I am still hungry

## At Dawn, Eyes Open / @ 40

tumbling over to-do lists, I am alert as
a hand trying at a combination lock
       [like the safe we now secret filled
       with adult-type documents or
       like my daughter's first locker]

amazing all of these numbers
—fitting together in concert—
         open doors
   I did not think possible
as I went elbow over elbow
on my belly         under imagined
spiky barbed wire
avoiding friendly and unfriendly fire
bright and displaced

jolted awake by the old walking-naked-
down-a-crowded-street dream, again
—oh, what rests in my heart—fever
laces my shoulders
[warm and soft like the green blanket
grandma bequeathed us]

      Young Girl, you couldn't know
that cinnamon will mellow in the bread
     that you will bake
for a family who will think
             you're the moon
that hunger will gnaw
like a fox worrying your hen's neck
enough to find sustenance from her brain
like the cord that wraps
         through your body
generating an electric hum
           steady as molasses

you will greet the sun
you will not squint

## The Spin Cycle / @ 20

You stack the quarters
in tall towers on the washing machine
during the spin cycle guessing which pile will first topple
while the delicates, synthetics, knits, and cottons
hit against the walls unbalanced.
Hot fabric smells, like holiday cooking,
comforting as you smooth wrinkles from khaki
crease pants as you fold
fumble with panties in front of strangers
slide bright bras in a hamper
mismatch socks.
A singular sock lies
in the bottom of the industrial drying machine
wooing a scrap of chewed yellowed paper.
You scrutinize the ink.
Smeared are numbers: three eight four six six five two—
a combination to a safe, which holds figures that would buy
Sal's Laundromat and Tanning Salon,
no, a social security number of
a success whose identity you could assume,
or a lotto number, yes, the winning ticket
if you just go to the VP and hand over
your dollar or your quarter into a phone machine if you'd call
if you call—an orthodontist, tax collector, video star,
mother, mayor, student, gas attendant, politician,
child, circus clown, a future, your future, the future...
The lost, no left, paper in your hand is soft like corduroy.
The pay phone is being used and this is ridiculous you are never that lucky
never that lucky leave the paper
leave the paper where you found it hidden
under the lost socks in the dryer.
But what if you did call
what if everyone called that number
would it be busy or would the answering machine click or would someone
answer and say,
*hello, I've been waiting for you...*

## Hang Dry / @ 40

Young Girl, you used to pick up calls
before you understood about solicitors,
wrong numbers, robocalls—that serendipity
flirts most with the prepared,
people positioned to throw a bag
over their shoulders and go.
Not the people who just talk adventure on their reels.
Now, you check for synthetic blends
before you'll purchase clothing
you can wear with the other things you own.
Pragmatic items that flex and bend
with your body—it's been years since you've unboxed
a pair of heels. Or ironed. Or dry cleaned.
Not out of laziness, but delicates take time,
extra care you don't find to give.
You'd rather shake a shirt loose,
straight out of your backpack,
pull it over your head
and move onto the next thing—
linger over moments,
not the instructions
for care.

*Barbara Susan, peony Robert F. Schmidt propagated the 1980s*

## Trichromatic Theory of Seeing

/

I'm learning about rods and cones and how the way my retinas
perceive red, blue, and green light, so when I survey a beach,
I sense nuances of blues: Superman ice cream, waves lazing
over a sandbar, the horizon line where deep ocean meets sky.
I'm learning the great blue whale, with only one type of cone,
doesn't see blue: her ocean, deep, monochromatic, pulses in
shades I can only guess at—our oceans dappled and moving
in ways that keep secrets, ways we cannot know or share.

//

In college, my grandfather, who was dichromatic, wrote me
a letter about a dream he had—he felt he dreamed in reds
and greens—the world in a thousand hues. He wrote a poem,
he was so taken with that waking moment when he *saw*
what he imagined I (we) see.

We called him
>*color blind.*

He was so eager to know the shades of the stop lights,
his beloved peonies. He could not explain to me in words
the color of my grandma's eyes. What he saw in my
patterned sweaters. Grandma decorated in pinks and greens.
He never complained—perhaps it felt like a 50s TV set,
comfortable greys and whites:

the contours,
the softness
>most important.

So many words passed between us in 46 years, but still
I cannot say what he saw when he took me to hunt seashells.

///


When I compare the remembered sunny yellow
of the coffee shop's siding on campus /20/ years
ago, where I was drafting poems, I don't think
it's the same shade now
        when we take my daughter for tea, though
the menu and chairs feel the same.
These new memories will be more butter yellow,
when we walk the uneven brick sidewalk
up to the porch and settle ourselves,
                              at least to my eyes.

*Tea break during alma mater visit*

## Dancing Silver Fish / @ 20

Yellow light
    dances on wet
        ripples. Resting on rocks,
            damp moss glitters. Bubbles,
        laced throughout green
    sludge, grip to
the stones
    as the water tugs
        at the moss' roots. Their small
            toes wiggle as they splash in
        the cool creek. Their bodies
    sit on the bent bank,
bellies heaving,
    as laughter tickles
        their young ribs. Fishing
            lines gleam a silver blue,
        transparent in the azure
    sky. Their lazy
poles arch
    blue and red,
        suspended in place by
            small hands carefully gripping the
        wet wood. Bologna
    dangles, from
stiff metal
    hooks over the half-
        foot deep surface.
            The creek parts as their slender
        ankles pull through
    the water in search
of a better
    spot on the bank
        where big silver trout
            would jump in the air, snapping
        at the bait on the end of
    each line, catching fast
to the rods
    straining below their tan faces.
        Mark tugs on his line.

        Teeth set; sandals firmly planted
      on the bank as he bends
    his elbows working
the line
    through the clear
      water. He holds up with
        pride the plump crawdad, clinging
    to the limp strip of
  pinkish brown
bologna,
    porous and bloated
      from soaking in the creek
        all afternoon. The small shell
      dangles in the draft
    exposed on the
swinging
    line. Mark's elf-
      like grin flashes in the
        sunlight as his thin fingers
      pop the pincers off the
    meat. Tossing the
crawdad
    back into the stream,
      they watch it slowly pass
        though the maze of rocks, disappearing
      under the dark shadows
    cast by the big bridge
where cars
    honk and speed by.

*Backyard pond, dug to water gardens and support critters*

*Goldfish in the backyard pond*

## Unobstructed Koi / @ 40

After you preserve your catch-and-
    release memory, after moving age 7,
        but before you will reconnect
            with Mark on social media 35 years
        later, you will catch
    yourself the kind of pain
you can't swallow,
    can't identify
        —a spit bait.
            Accident will force you
        to your knees, Young Girl—crush you
    in a place no one will notice.
You will crawl on a boat dock
    to a short pillar
        and pull yourself up.
            You will contemplate what carp must feel
        when their fins disintegrate,
    and water passes where it shouldn't.
You will quickly learn
    to brace yourself.
        You will shuffle your protesting body
            plank by plank until your toes touch sunlight.
        When the air is sweeter,
    you will shake off a faint,
see bright carp
    hauling their bodies through muck
        in figure eights.
            You will remember the crawdad's imagined
        relief to plunge back
    to the creek's belly
after surfacing with the morsel,
    the unexpected meal.
        You will remember the cool
            shade of the bridge, no that dock,
        the bright light dancing like silver fish
    on the pond's surface under the dock's roof.
You will question,
    you will question

     happy endings, lazy afternoons
       playing by creek beds, carp trapped
     in weeds, trout moving upstream.
  Hope, like the sun, will burn hot
in your veins. You will tell
   yourself to beat circles, move forward,
     find a current. For the second time,
      you will know
   you've got to do something,
   like the crawdad clinging to meat,
anything but sink.
   You'll learn you must tread water:
       yet, in that moment
       you'll remain still.

## The Day My Dog Died / @ 20

Ricky poked it with a stick,
pronouncing him *dead meat.*
Heat from the asphalt rose
and sat on his belly and our shoulders.
A ripe smell, similar to
Mr. Thompson's garbage bags,
bullied through our nostrils, and Jenny
tumbled onto the curb in a melodramatic way
crying about her *loss of innocence.* Sarah
said she was *going to puke.*

The blue sky's glare on the road
made me squint, and puddles seemed
to take my attention away from
the golden legs patiently erect,
waiting as if he had a question…
we wondered if it had rained the night before.

Ricky threw a rock at his face
*yep,* he said, *it was toast.*
Jenny wailed—*we should call the police.*
Sarah walked to Mrs. Waitz's azaleas
and vomited lunch. A plane's shadow sped
over our heads and those puddles vanished
—my dog lay still as Ricky stepped on its tail.
*It's not going anywhere,* he said
scratching his left armpit.

Jenny stood up and rubbed her fists
in her red eyes. Sarah kicked a rock
with her sandal, stalling at the curb,
her pink T-shirt sticking to
her narrow frame in the heat.
And I remembered I didn't own a dog.
That Spike, Randy, Spot, Bailey…waited,
legs in air for someone to call his name aloud—
but the buzz of lawn mowers muffled any silence.

**the day our cat died / reflecting @ 40**

later   (after the call during grad school)      after I'd swept soiled tissues from the nightstand     and stood (hugging)     the wire basket against my chest,
      which hopped and pushed    (b r e a t h e)    through plugged nostrils   I remembered you wrote that poem, Young Girl   (a scene really) about some kids' (you never knew) responses to a dog's carcass (you never saw)
      you wrote it before *this* moment        but after your family's cat was   *given to a new family*   in elementary school     one that
    *could take better care of him*
                before you understood what that *really meant*
but the years
    (those years) had already dulled that young heartache    like a riverstone   (maybe one you'd picked up on a walk in the woods)    one you could hold
        (that understanding)    in your palm    (find comfort)

*you* didn't have to make the decision to  *put*   *him*      *d o w n*

when you wrote about Ricky and the dead dog     you knew bearing
 witness
   to the death of any pet    (b e l o v e d)    would make your heart beat faster   explode like dandelion seeds in the wind   love   scattershot
    and      splintered    (embedded in all things that follow)

now (after this second call)  I still cringe when I see soft fur curled or crushed
      on a road a sidewalk a ditch a parking lot the curb by someone's home
because after the call you     (no)    after *we* got the call   we stopped short
because we didn't know    (you didn't recognize grief then, Young Girl)
that such a short,
    soft life
        could leave
        such—

                                                      hollowness

*Our current roommate, Peanut*

**(nearsighted)**

I reject *myopic* at the eye doctor's office.
I appreciate my eyes are aging: I squint
at smaller neighborhood street signs, blame
color contrast. (Know I'm breaking down.)
But words matter, and while I reflect on

light bouncing off objects, the electrical
signals my brain interprets the light to be,
vanity has me holding my creativity in high
esteem: even with my astigmatism, I would
discern patterns (and narratives) in the old

Magic Eye puzzles. Sight is thought to be
humans' strongest sense, how we engage
with our worlds uniquely. My lenses help
refract light making its way to my retinas,
washing my landscape in watercolor hues:

today is muted by rainclouds and brightened
by daffodils in the greening yard. Water-
soaked leaf litter hints at a storm brewing,
and I tuck my grandmother's umbrella,
blue with yellow flowers, under my elbow.

When I focus on just the next moment, there
is a warm feeling of control: as I shift my attention
to the horizon, everything's less clear, less known,
and that haze, what's unexpected, sits curled
in a cold, fetal ball in my stomach's pit.

## Cycles on Wood Street / @ 20

Always, I must change the toilet paper
roll while sitting on the sweating john above
Wood Street. I hear morning.
Amos collects tin cans     clank
click clankyclank          lids hit
metal pouring debris—Mrs. Shellman's
moldy pot pie lands on faded
*New York Times,* tampon, old
socks, salad dressing bottle, toothpaste,
parking ticket, tissues—nose blows
next door, a thick sound like the tuba
player across the street in apartment
310 practicing on Wednesday afternoons.
Mr. Gadston gargles through the heat grate.
Cold breeze from my open window makes
goosebumps pop on my tummy, rolling
over my belly button, and pushes shower
steam under the old squeaky door.
Taxis screech from the curb destination
anyplace where coffee percolates.
Whishwhirl scratch of the street sweeper
follows their wake while worried mothers holler
downstairs for kids to wake for school buses.
Pigeons whisper on telephone wires
coohoot          twipwhip          knoby-knees
John and Garry and D. Parker call me
Knobby-knees, my elbows rest on them.
Burr-ring Dad's alarm goes in the bedroom.
Soft cardboard taps the plastic dispenser,
as I pull toilet paper from the wall slowly.
Knock knock     tap     slap     knock
on the squeaky door—*Just a minute, Dad.*
Second swipe—*Oh my God.*
Beet red sticky smoothing sliding
beating on the squeaky door—I think I am dying.
hurry rush flush   my cheeks flush
water spits and sprays hard from the tap
scrub my hands with lava soap lather

Smacking of cupboards and cabinets—*I've got to shave,*
*please finish up in there, Honey.*
Only old Easter bathroom napkins
company wipe their fingers on at the holidays
can be found —what-am-I-going-to-do—
warm white underpants moist.
I throw the door open and its hinges squeak.
*Daddy, you've got to go to the store now. Please.*
*But it's seven thirty, and I'm in my bathrobe.*
Tears spring to my eyes and the toaster spurts
toast. Mom butters and calls softly
wise to my plea from the pink-tiled bathroom.
*Jake, get your jacket Sweet-thing needs—*
the steam whistle sounds from the tea kettle.

## Cycles on Wind Street / @ 40

So, you're still changing toilet paper rolls,
Young Girl—that hasn't changed—but now
there's no shyness, talking of menstruation
without assonance, without setting a scene.
You can laugh now about that birthday night,
just turned 14: how the shock of beet red
nipped at the heels of embarrassment, when
your little sister announced before the sleep
over, *is she going to stain the sheets?* It's easy,
like folding fitted sheets, preparing annual taxes,
finding time to wash baseboards—the origin story
rolls off your tongue, settles at strangers' feet,
even your daughter's. Impatient, you expected
to transform, like butterfly from cocoon, but
no, it was merely a new routine, the peeling
of plastic, the wearing of dark shorts, maybe
a decision to sit on the beach—summertime
littered with sanitary napkins, but you
ever-blooming, taking little notice of menses
flooding what would make you a mother:
blessed sensory overload at five in the morning.
What you cannot talk about now, 30 years later,
is the moment mensuration morphed: your hair
falling out in clumps, erratic bleeding, weighted
mammary glands, pain zippering your abdomen,
when you'd always been, *Normal*. Balding, bent
double on an exam table, you observe your ovaries
on grainy film six months after your fortieth birthday
holding your breath, reading ultrasounds like tea
leaves, until the technician says, *off the record,
I'd say you look normal,* because she knows it's
not easy—like coordinating the family's schedule,
remembering to change the furnace filter,
finding time to dust baseboards—your aging body
transforms, like ants under cordyceps' control,
new routines for middle age. Impatient, you
will learn to tend your evolving body, cultivate
its cycles. Young Girl, hair grows back slowly.

*Beets from the garden*

## Rush Hour Rant / @ 20

the low orange sun stammers as clouds
roll on the blue horizon faster than dice in Vegas
street traffic chatter pushes and pours
through the small crack in the Escort's window
squeezing my aggravation like a showgirl's
tight lace garter

                blank noise
infiltrates until there is no longer room
inside the car to take deep breaths
with you smirking in the passenger seat
squeeze me instead with these collaborated comforts
        Charmin, Evian, Irish Spring,
        Kleenex Plus, Downy Fresh, Snuggle—
bombard me with soothing anecdotes like
            the singing caged bird set free
    will return if meant to be singing, or perhaps,
  gagging on Hallmark adjectives, which burn
in my throat—I will vomit platitudes in plentitude
when purging my soul of…good will towards a man
filled with false prophecy I will sing to you
    *everything is going to be okay*
as I clutch warm worn leather on the steering
wheel

      call me Isaiah and I will tell you
which way to proceed        curves ahead
                            dead end  one way  children
                            playing  slippery when wet  stop

stopped in the lot next to Nevada Ned's Bar and Grill
I elude your grasp as your hand caresses my knee
evasive as silk stockings, I am transparent
only when you stretch pull twist puncture
I am nude   I am sandlefoot    I am suntan
I am the androgynous legs of a dancer
springing  twirling  prancing  leaping away from you
under hot neon electric lights

### Deck Dining Rant / @ 40

the midwestern sun sits on the trees as gnats
search sweat on the deck, determined as toddlers
gasoline blowers and lawn mowers roar and bellow
drowning out conversation over corn cobs
squeezing my aggravation like loppers
on the witch hazel limbs

                         buzzing noise
and gnats blanket us until hands are swiping
air between bites, waving away conversation
      we are distracted at the tiled table
console me instead with nature's noises
      blue bird, tree frog, cicada
      branches scraping siding, soft rain—
or stoke me with neighborhood idioms like
           hustle and bustle, hot air, blow one's horn
      or, perhaps, burn one's fossil fuel at high volume
   gag on fumes that dissipate as driveways
lose their shag, grasses get crew cuts—I hear them
striving for plastic fantastic perfection    no blade
      out of place    no blemish fouling
clean lines   evergreen hedges   full-width rollers' lines
dreamhouses drenched in
      clothianidin   thiamethoxam   imidacloprid
so ants won't trespass in coordinated
rows

      bring me the buzz of bees
riots of perennial flowers           rows of runner beans
           cherry tomatoes  beetroot  swiss chard
           unruly squash  marigolds  lemon thyme

dishes cleared   deck cleared   watering can in hand
I douse the garden at dusk so droplets have time to dive deep
into sub soil   escaping the rough din that won't diminish 'til after dark
      We are soil     We are water   We are warm summer air
We are caretaking porous borders, Young Girl,
                mycelium binding us

*Commute to the high school for Hattie's extracurriculars*

**night vision**

there is little darkness, like the dark of caves when
flashlights are extinguished and it's hard to know
what's real. Caves' cold kisses keep me alert, and
as my 100 million sensitive light cells rest, my mind
images what must be, or not be, there—taking liberty
to create. At night, when our orange tabby walks
on my bladder or a dream prods my consciousness
to wake, my pupils expand to take in the streetlight
beams that sneak between the curtain and rod,
the green glow from a device left plugged in, and
a full moon that's bathed the backyard in a halo,
light I step in, patch by patch, on the rug, making
my way to the bathroom. I see our cat's eyes flash
in moonlight, the tapetum luciduman shining amber
gold watching me fumble in semi-dark, unfocused,
in the sleeping house. He's amused, except for when
I miss him shift positions and nearly stumble on him
on the way back to bed. It's easy to dismiss nighttime
stumbles, the world muted and sleepy in the nearly-
dark, woven with dreamscapes, worries, and shadows.
In the commute's sunlight, pupils constrict; scientists
tell me my brain lights up, circuits thrum, my circadian
clock resets, cortisol pumps—Young Girl, morning is
still our time when the world seems ready to conquer,
the horizon sharp, the task-at-hand focused. I see
pictures of you, eyes wide, glowing red, and know its
blood vessels reflecting the flash, soul ablaze, young
love warming our heart, the glow emanating through
our eyes. When I think of memories and dreams driving
to work, of night fumbles and love, it is with a smile
soft around the edges like looped cotton in moonlight.

*Clouds cover full moon over backyard*

*@ 20 / So do you use safe sex?*

                              the woman asks me.
She smells like lavender and wears purple, a wool scarf
wrapped around her white hair and neck.
I bounce on brown vinyl sitting next to her on the G bus.

Excuse me? I slowly pull ear muffs from my head
and grab the seat railing, bracing for the curve.
She slides towards me on the seat and winks.
Slick under the bus' wheels; the tires spin quickly
grabbing at pavement two inches below snow.
*Do you?* She smiles timidly.

Well, I…I grip the railing. She glances around
the muggy bus and, leaning, whispers to me,
*I just met a man at the VFW last night.* Her face reddens.
And you want to know if I have sex?
*Oh my, I guess I didn't even introduce…You see
he propositioned me…*she giggles. Ding.

The bus slows to the curb, a man in a blue sock hat climbs
down the steps, his breath billows in the air
white as her hair, which leans towards me fervently.
*Hello, I'm Maggie. I would have asked my best friend Meg,
I really haven't done this in such a long time.*
Her cheeks blush and the woman with groceries coughs twice.

Yes, I nod, glancing at the passengers' faces watching
pavement while dividing lines melt into a continuous white line.
Her aroma winds around my memories and I think of
Grandma asking a stranger on the bus about sex.
Grandpa's been gone too long and she's all dressed up, going to the VFW.
Maggie opens her brown leather purse and pulls out
faded photographs grinning. *See this was Meg.*

She looks lovely. I hold the photo tenderly
in my mitten. Meg's dead and Maggie's asking me
how to love the VFW man. Ding. Ding. Ding.
I pick up my bag and look at Maggie's worn gloves.

I have to get off at the next stop, Maggie.
Her mahogany eyes look past me at the MTV ad
on the chipped luggage rack. Ding.
*What bus is this?* This is the G bus, Maggie.

*Cherry harvest*

### @ 40 / Don't you think she's dressed like a whore?

                                                                     the woman asks me.
We're both wiping sweat with white towels, breathing heavy
as we wait at the gym's water fountain. We've seen each other
in cardio class—until it strained my back, and I strapped
my brace on, which hides beneath an old T-shirt and baggy
purple soccer shorts (the ones you got in high school, Young Girl).

Pardon? I make a show of removing my ear buds, giving her
a chance to revise the question. I assume she's referencing
the young woman with Barbie-doll curves bending too long
over the middle-school-style fountain.

This woman has thick yoga pants that flare, bright white New
Balances with pink laces, and a three-quarter sleeved high
performance shirt that's not wicking quickly enough.
*Do you?* She says, a little too loudly.

Are you still in the morning cardio class? I ask. We watch
the young woman flip her ponytail and hit her towel against
a young man's chest. *What? No.* She clicks her tongue.
*It's like decorum's gone out the window.* The line moves.
*Remember when gym uniforms went from here
to here?* We got to wear clothes from home, I say.
I consider my daughter now wears a similar uniform.
This water break isn't as restful as I'd hoped.
(You, Young Girl, were lucky you got to choose.)

*Hmm.* She nods, looking me over, and I wonder if she can
see the torso's metal buckles through the thin cotton and
what I might be hiding. She smooths the hem of her shirt.

*What passes as exercise clothing now should*—she stops,
purses her lips, readying for her drink. I watch as she gracefully
bends towards the fountain, a different kind of fanfare that still
draws attention. Athleticism. Confidence. Grace. She gives me
a knowing look as she turns, heads towards the treadmills.

She doesn't know, Young Girl, many accidents ago, I once wore my torso brace outside my T-shirts, before I learned snagging its loops on equipment handles hurts. A lot. Now, I dress for pain, repetition, sweat. Not modesty.

## 87 ° F / @ 20

Your voice was
the swift sharp curve of a southern brook
pouring into the sea
muggy heat sitting on the silver blue wet
stilted air calm and green
You were the first streak of lightning
crackling
like fried chicken sizzling in a skillet
Your breading thick
layers of flesh hiding desires
like the weave of a sweater
intense patterns
they zigzagged around strong shoulders
knotted wool matted along the collar
soft    comforting
warm like the cab of a pickup truck
in summer
the blurry air of distorted heat
drifting
off the radiator

## 98.6 ° F / @ 40

His voice is still strong
as an estuary's current in the dark
hospital room before dawn
rich like crema topping espresso
He is still a metronome
breathe in   hold   breathe out
steady as a clock ticking in a kitchen
His voice warms
like Sunday pancakes topped
with apples and cinnamon
sweet like the blanket,
Young Girl,
we wrapped our daughter in
little peach flowers dotted in a cream field
soft   comforting
home like the first store-bought sofa
cushions stacked
His hand resting on my swollen belly
waiting
patiently for family

*Early evening strawberry harvest*

## TBD

I picked an occupation grounded in foresight:
the kind a gardener uses to anticipate which
amendments the soil will need the coming
season or cultivating transferable career skills,
not the kind that predicts wealth, love, baldness.

In the yearly crops of young people discovering
themselves and their paths forward, themes
emerge—and we take care to prepare for futures
based on expert projections, what we think might
lead to lives they feel will fuel their best selves.

I am learning that I cannot know when cucurbit
beetles will settle on zucchini or deer will top
tomatoes or spring rains will mildew roses,
no matter the amendments we applied based on
last season. I would not have guessed my taste

mid-life for the allium family, calendula, or
horseradish. When I think of my sixties, I imagine
preparing for who I am now in a sixties landscape,
but I cannot know what I will grow in my garden,
who I will be, how to prepare—

Young Girl, I see you @ 20, I see me @ 40, and
I see how we've changed; I still see your blueprint.
I imagine @60 I will savor May strawberries,
though I cannot know where the patches will grow.
Preparation with care, however incomplete, is comfort.

## Portrait of Longing on Highway 31 / @ 20

Dusk and the dog stands,
black ears forward on
her head, in the green ditch.
Rose creeps over
the wheat field to the west.
South on 31
traffic rushes by and
pushes warm gusts
against her chest. Absently
she shifts weight from right
paw to left. The trucks'
horns blast, shaking
her body, and disappear
around the gray bend.
Patiently she waits
as shadows grow black
on the pavement, whispering
in her attentive ears that
it is time to move on.

Ten yards further,
on the shoulder, lies black
bulk. His fur dances
in the wind, pushed from swift
cars speeding wildly.
His muscles are lax,
as though he slumbers on the gravel.
He did not follow her,
tumbling into the ditch after
braving the break in loud
automobiles on the highway.
She swallows rapid breaths
waiting for him to jump
up from the ground. He
will come after resting
and she will lick the red
from his cold dark nose.

# Portrait of Mourning in the Coop / @ 40

The hens coo softly,
my dear Young Girl,
low in their throats
like your quiet sobs
in the dormitory when
you first learned your
grandfather died.
They know too: death
is quick on sunny days
whether foraging worms
or reading in lawn chairs.

Three hawks who'd
been stalking the flock
patiently for weeks—
an untended moment,
all our guards down.
Imagine their alarm,
duck and cover, sisters
racing under pines,
into their shed, through
low arbor vitae and
talons quietly tearing
chests, wings, throats
—downy underfeathers
floating in chill air.

It is silent when we
head to collect eggs
that were not laid, see
white, black, brown
feathers littering the yard,
carcasses discarded
unceremoniously. It is
silent like the dark ride
to the airport for your
solo flight to his memorial.
Silence until the two hens

coo in the coop, comforting
each other in a corner,
a dirge for their sisters.
They know too: death
is quick to leave silence,
proprioception wheeling,
readjusting to absence—
sadness low in the throat
slow to escape.

*Ladies at dusk*

## Wedding Ring Pattern / @ 20

While lying beneath
patches of bright cotton
subdued by the dark,

faint shadows etch nostalgic
shapes on the wall.
Behind eyelids I can see

the silhouette of your face.
Nighttime conjures the hum
of your exhales syncopated

with the running radiator.
I cannot distinguish the
curve of your shoulder

from the quilt's exhausted sag
as it cradles the sleepy feather pillow
your head once rested on.

**Log Cabin Pattern / @ 40**

While smoothing wrinkles
from blocks of soft flannel
lit by the sun,

I remember his hand
twining mine.
New rings glinting in

late afternoon. Hands cutting
rectangles, building squares
in solid rows together.

Tonight, we will pull this
thick quilt over weary shoulders,
bend our bodies into a crescent

moon before our home's lullaby
of rushing air and ticking clocks
hushes us to sleep.

*Wedding Ring quilt my mother, Kathy Kershner, made to celebrate our 20th anniversary*

### Electrical impulses, that's all

the optometrist casually says, *and everyone interprets
the impulses in their own way.* We can't know if we see
exactly the same objects, same shades, same shadows—
our eyes turn the light reflecting off them into electrical
impulses that our brains sort out. A headache is building
thinking about what orange *means*, this sumo citrus
orange that feels bumpy and bulbus in my palm and
wet, sweet in my mouth. A honey sweet, not a cane sugar
sweet, if our tongues both discern the difference in the
same, orangy way? I'm distracted thinking Matrix-like
thoughts, and the new car warns me as I head towards
the dashed white line that there's something in my blind
spot. I thought I'd checked, but sweep the mirrors again,
the rearviews showing the SUV's already sped forward.
People interpret the world differently. Those moments
our vision or view is obstructed by something—blinders or
blind spots—other senses fill in information, the sumo's
bump/fragrance/sweet. Young Girl, I can't remember
what input made you put strings of words into lines.
But I appreciate your trying to capture each moment
for me, as I do now for our future self, as energy fades,
impulses weaken, skin dries, song lyrics are forgotten,
and flavor fades in a mouth, worn from telling tales.

## Acknowledgments

I'd like to thank Maura Stanton and David Wojahn who helped me start my poetry path at Indiana University. Many thanks to Richard Cecil and Donald J. Gray who provided exceptional support and mentorship during my senior honors thesis, the poetry manuscript from /my 20s/ that is excerpted here. Poets Kylie Seitz and Shauna Sartoris, who I worked with more recently in workshops at the University of Indianapolis, provided valuable feedback on the poems written /in my 40s/. I thank them for their insights. I am grateful for the support of my family as we grow together. Hattie Mae, thank you for your notes.

A hearty thanks to Dr. Diana Prljevic and Eyes on Main staff in Carmel, IN, especially Kimberly Peters who coordinated a photoshoot for cover images.

And, thank you to the magazines who published previous versions of these poems:

"Hindsight is 20/40" & "The Spin Cycle at 20." *Pirene's Fountain,* vol. 16, iss. 24, 2023, p. 71 & pp. 72-73.
"Deck Dining Rant." *Last Leaves,* Issue 5: Growth, 31 October 2022, p. 150. https://www.lastleavesmag.com/last-leaves-issues.
"Cycles on Wind Street." *The Scores,* issue 10, Aug. 2021, https://thescores.org.uk/liz-whiteacre/.
"Upon Closing My Eyes at 20." & "At Dawn, 40-Year-Old Eyes Open." *The Last Stanza,* no. 6, 21 Sept. 2021, p. 12.
"Portrait of Mourning in the Coop." *Flying Island Journal,* vol. 8, no. 21, August 2021, https://www.flyingislandjournal.org/2021/08/portrait-of-mourning-in-coop-poem-by.html.

@ 20, Liz wrote these poems as a student at Indiana University, where she majored in English and Criminal Justice. She went on to get her MFA in creative writing at Southern Illinois University and later married her college sweetheart. Now, @ 40, **Liz Whiteacre** is a Professor of English at the University of Indianapolis. Her poetry has appeared in *Kaleidoscope, Wordgathering, Disability Studies Quarterly, Breath and Shadow,* and other literary magazines. She is the author of *Hit the Ground* and *it could account for the panic.*

www.ingramcontent.com/pod-product-compliance
Lightning Source LLC
Chambersburg PA
CBHW040253170426
43191CB00019B/2403